50 Premium Cheese Dishes

By: Kelly Johnson

Table of Contents

- Baked Brie with Honey and Almonds
- Truffle Mac and Cheese
- Lobster and Gruyère Ravioli
- Brie and Prosciutto Stuffed Chicken
- Raclette with Roasted Vegetables
- Fettuccine Alfredo with Parmesan
- Pappardelle with Blue Cheese and Walnuts
- Gorgonzola and Pear Tart
- Caprese Salad with Burrata
- Three-Cheese Pizza with Truffle Oil
- Cheese Fondue with Artisan Bread
- Spinach and Ricotta Stuffed Shells
- Baked Goat Cheese with Tomato Basil Sauce
- Lobster Thermidor with Gruyère
- Brie and Mushroom Stuffed Beef Wellington
- Grilled Cheese with Caramelized Onion and Gruyère
- Baked Ziti with Ricotta and Mozzarella
- Macaroni and Cheese with Smoked Gouda
- Ricotta and Spinach Gnocchi
- Parmesan-Crusted Halibut
- Manchego and Quince Jam Crostini
- Mozzarella di Bufala with Roasted Tomatoes
- Burrata with Fresh Basil and Olive Oil
- Truffle and Parmesan Fries
- Stuffed Piquillo Peppers with Goat Cheese
- Cheddar and Ale Soup
- Burrata and Prosciutto Salad
- Feta and Olive Tapenade on Crostini
- Goat Cheese and Beets Salad
- Creamy Spinach and Feta Dip
- Lobster and Shrimp Macaroni and Cheese
- Chicken Parmesan with Fresh Mozzarella
- Grilled Halloumi with Lemon and Mint
- Baked Eggplant Parmesan with Fresh Mozzarella
- Sweet Potato and Goat Cheese Tart

- Ricotta and Lemon Cannoli
- Roquefort and Walnut Salad
- Grilled Steak with Blue Cheese Butter
- Moussaka with Feta Cheese
- Ricotta and Spinach Stuffed Chicken Breast
- Cheese-Stuffed Poblano Peppers
- Focaccia with Ricotta and Honey
- Parmesan and Herb-Crusted Chicken
- Truffle Gouda Risotto
- Prosciutto and Brie Croissants
- Poached Pears with Gorgonzola and Walnuts
- Sautéed Shrimp with Garlic and Parmesan
- Grilled Veggie and Goat Cheese Sandwich
- Baked Polenta with Blue Cheese and Mushrooms
- Crab Cakes with Parmesan Cream Sauce

Baked Brie with Honey and Almonds

Ingredients:

- 1 wheel of Brie cheese (8 oz)
- 1/4 cup sliced almonds
- 2 tbsp honey
- Fresh thyme or rosemary for garnish (optional)

Instructions:

1. Preheat the oven to 350°F (175°C).
2. Place the Brie wheel on a baking sheet lined with parchment paper.
3. Sprinkle the sliced almonds evenly over the top of the Brie.
4. Drizzle the honey over the almonds and cheese.
5. Bake for 10-12 minutes, or until the cheese is soft and slightly melted.
6. Garnish with fresh thyme or rosemary. Serve with crackers, fruit, or toasted baguette slices.

Truffle Mac and Cheese

Ingredients:

- 8 oz elbow macaroni
- 2 tbsp butter
- 2 tbsp flour
- 1 1/2 cups whole milk
- 1 cup heavy cream
- 2 cups sharp cheddar cheese, shredded
- 1 cup Gruyère cheese, shredded
- 2 tbsp truffle oil
- Salt and pepper to taste
- 1/4 cup grated Parmesan cheese
- 1 tbsp fresh parsley, chopped (optional)

Instructions:

1. Cook the macaroni according to package directions. Drain and set aside.
2. In a large saucepan, melt the butter over medium heat. Stir in the flour and cook for 1-2 minutes.
3. Slowly add the milk and cream, whisking continuously until the mixture thickens.
4. Stir in the cheddar and Gruyère cheese, then season with salt and pepper.
5. Once the cheese is melted and smooth, add the cooked macaroni and toss to coat.
6. Drizzle in the truffle oil and mix.
7. Transfer to a serving dish, sprinkle with Parmesan, and garnish with fresh parsley. Serve immediately.

Lobster and Gruyère Ravioli

Ingredients:

- 8 oz fresh or frozen lobster meat, chopped
- 1/4 cup ricotta cheese
- 1/4 cup Gruyère cheese, grated
- 1 egg (for the filling)
- 1/2 tsp lemon zest
- Salt and pepper to taste
- 1 package fresh pasta dough (or homemade)
- 4 tbsp butter
- 2 cloves garlic, minced
- 1/4 cup fresh parsley, chopped
- Lemon wedges for serving

Instructions:

1. In a bowl, combine the lobster, ricotta, Gruyère, egg, lemon zest, salt, and pepper. Mix well to form the filling.
2. Roll out the pasta dough and cut into squares. Place a small spoonful of the lobster mixture in the center of each square.
3. Fold the pasta over to form a triangle or rectangle and press the edges to seal.
4. Bring a pot of salted water to a boil. Gently drop the ravioli into the water and cook for 4-5 minutes, or until they float to the surface.
5. In a large pan, melt the butter over medium heat. Add the garlic and sauté for 1 minute until fragrant.
6. Add the cooked ravioli to the pan and toss gently in the garlic butter.
7. Sprinkle with fresh parsley and serve with lemon wedges.

Brie and Prosciutto Stuffed Chicken

Ingredients:

- 4 boneless, skinless chicken breasts
- 4 oz Brie cheese, sliced
- 4 slices prosciutto
- 2 tbsp olive oil
- 1 tsp fresh rosemary, chopped
- Salt and pepper to taste

Instructions:

1. Preheat the oven to 375°F (190°C).
2. Carefully slice a pocket into the side of each chicken breast.
3. Stuff each pocket with slices of Brie and prosciutto.
4. Heat olive oil in a skillet over medium heat. Season the chicken breasts with rosemary, salt, and pepper.
5. Brown the chicken in the skillet for 3-4 minutes on each side.
6. Transfer the chicken to the oven and bake for 15-20 minutes, or until the chicken is cooked through and the cheese is melted.
7. Serve with a side of roasted vegetables or a simple salad.

Raclette with Roasted Vegetables

Ingredients:

- 1 lb small potatoes, halved
- 2 cups Brussels sprouts, halved
- 1 bell pepper, sliced
- 1 zucchini, sliced
- 2 tbsp olive oil
- Salt and pepper to taste
- 8 oz Raclette cheese, sliced
- Fresh parsley for garnish

Instructions:

1. Preheat the oven to 400°F (200°C).
2. Toss the potatoes, Brussels sprouts, bell pepper, and zucchini in olive oil, salt, and pepper. Spread them out on a baking sheet.
3. Roast the vegetables for 25-30 minutes, or until tender and golden, stirring halfway through.
4. While the vegetables are roasting, melt the Raclette cheese over the vegetables using a raclette grill or in an oven-safe dish under the broiler.
5. Serve the vegetables topped with melted cheese and garnish with fresh parsley.

Fettuccine Alfredo with Parmesan

Ingredients:

- 8 oz fettuccine pasta
- 1/2 cup unsalted butter
- 1 cup heavy cream
- 2 cups Parmesan cheese, grated
- 2 cloves garlic, minced
- Salt and pepper to taste
- Fresh parsley, chopped for garnish

Instructions:

1. Cook the fettuccine according to package instructions. Drain, reserving some pasta water.
2. In a large pan, melt the butter over medium heat. Add the garlic and sauté for 1 minute.
3. Pour in the heavy cream and bring to a simmer. Cook for 2-3 minutes, until slightly thickened.
4. Stir in the Parmesan cheese and season with salt and pepper.
5. Add the cooked fettuccine to the pan, tossing to coat in the sauce. If the sauce is too thick, add some reserved pasta water.
6. Garnish with fresh parsley and serve immediately.

Pappardelle with Blue Cheese and Walnuts

Ingredients:

- 8 oz pappardelle pasta
- 2 tbsp olive oil
- 1/2 cup blue cheese, crumbled
- 1/4 cup walnuts, toasted and chopped
- 1/2 cup heavy cream
- Salt and pepper to taste
- Fresh thyme for garnish

Instructions:

1. Cook the pappardelle according to package instructions. Drain, reserving some pasta water.
2. In a pan, heat the olive oil over medium heat. Add the blue cheese and heavy cream, stirring to melt the cheese into the cream.
3. Add the cooked pasta to the pan, tossing to combine. If the sauce is too thick, add some reserved pasta water to reach desired consistency.
4. Stir in the toasted walnuts and season with salt and pepper.
5. Garnish with fresh thyme and serve.

Gorgonzola and Pear Tart

Ingredients:

- 1 sheet puff pastry
- 1/2 cup Gorgonzola cheese, crumbled
- 2 pears, sliced
- 1 tbsp honey
- Fresh thyme for garnish

Instructions:

1. Preheat the oven to 375°F (190°C).
2. Roll out the puff pastry on a baking sheet lined with parchment paper.
3. Spread the Gorgonzola cheese evenly over the pastry, leaving a border around the edges.
4. Arrange the pear slices on top of the cheese.
5. Drizzle with honey and bake for 15-20 minutes, or until the pastry is golden and crisp.
6. Garnish with fresh thyme and serve warm.

Caprese Salad with Burrata

Ingredients:

- 4 ripe tomatoes, sliced
- 8 oz Burrata cheese
- Fresh basil leaves
- 2 tbsp olive oil
- 1 tbsp balsamic vinegar
- Salt and pepper to taste

Instructions:

1. Arrange the tomato slices on a serving platter.
2. Tear the Burrata into pieces and place over the tomatoes.
3. Sprinkle fresh basil leaves over the salad.
4. Drizzle with olive oil and balsamic vinegar.
5. Season with salt and pepper, and serve immediately.

Three-Cheese Pizza with Truffle Oil

Ingredients:

- 1 pizza dough (store-bought or homemade)
- 1/2 cup mozzarella cheese, shredded
- 1/2 cup fontina cheese, shredded
- 1/2 cup goat cheese, crumbled
- 1 tbsp truffle oil
- 1/4 cup fresh basil, chopped
- Olive oil for brushing
- Salt and pepper to taste

Instructions:

1. Preheat the oven to 475°F (245°C).
2. Roll out the pizza dough onto a baking sheet or pizza stone.
3. Sprinkle the mozzarella, fontina, and goat cheese evenly across the dough.
4. Drizzle truffle oil over the cheese, and season with salt and pepper.
5. Bake the pizza for 10-12 minutes, or until the crust is golden and the cheese is melted and bubbly.
6. Remove from the oven and sprinkle with fresh basil. Slice and serve.

Cheese Fondue with Artisan Bread

Ingredients:

- 8 oz Gruyère cheese, shredded
- 8 oz Emmental cheese, shredded
- 1 clove garlic, halved
- 1 cup dry white wine
- 1 tbsp lemon juice
- 1 tsp cornstarch
- 2 tbsp kirsch (cherry brandy) or water
- Freshly ground black pepper
- Freshly grated nutmeg
- Artisan bread, cubed (for dipping)

Instructions:

1. Rub the inside of a fondue pot with the halved garlic clove.
2. In a small bowl, mix the cornstarch with kirsch or water to make a slurry.
3. Pour the wine and lemon juice into the pot and heat gently over low heat.
4. Gradually add the shredded cheeses, stirring constantly until melted and smooth.
5. Stir in the cornstarch mixture, and cook for 2-3 minutes until thickened.
6. Season with black pepper and nutmeg.
7. Serve with cubed artisan bread for dipping.

Spinach and Ricotta Stuffed Shells

Ingredients:

- 12 jumbo pasta shells
- 2 cups fresh spinach, chopped
- 1 1/2 cups ricotta cheese
- 1 cup mozzarella cheese, shredded
- 1/2 cup Parmesan cheese, grated
- 1 egg, beaten
- 1 tsp garlic powder
- 1 tsp dried oregano
- 2 cups marinara sauce
- Fresh basil, chopped (optional)

Instructions:

1. Preheat the oven to 375°F (190°C).
2. Cook the pasta shells according to package directions. Drain and set aside.
3. In a bowl, mix the spinach, ricotta, mozzarella, Parmesan, egg, garlic powder, and oregano.
4. Stuff each pasta shell with the spinach and ricotta mixture.
5. Spread half of the marinara sauce on the bottom of a baking dish.
6. Arrange the stuffed shells in the dish and top with the remaining marinara sauce.
7. Bake for 25-30 minutes, until bubbly and golden.
8. Garnish with fresh basil and serve.

Baked Goat Cheese with Tomato Basil Sauce

Ingredients:

- 8 oz goat cheese log
- 1 cup marinara sauce
- 1/4 cup fresh basil, chopped
- 1 tbsp olive oil
- Salt and pepper to taste
- Crusty bread or crackers for serving

Instructions:

1. Preheat the oven to 375°F (190°C).
2. Place the goat cheese log in a baking dish.
3. Pour the marinara sauce over the cheese and season with salt and pepper.
4. Drizzle olive oil over the top and sprinkle with fresh basil.
5. Bake for 20-25 minutes, until the cheese is soft and the sauce is bubbling.
6. Serve with crusty bread or crackers for dipping.

Lobster Thermidor with Gruyère

Ingredients:

- 2 lobster tails
- 1 tbsp butter
- 1/2 cup shallots, finely chopped
- 1/4 cup brandy (such as Cognac)
- 1/2 cup heavy cream
- 1/4 cup Gruyère cheese, shredded
- 2 tbsp fresh parsley, chopped
- Salt and pepper to taste
- 1 tbsp breadcrumbs (optional)

Instructions:

1. Preheat the oven to 400°F (200°C).
2. Boil the lobster tails in salted water for 6-8 minutes. Drain and set aside to cool.
3. Remove the lobster meat from the shells and chop it into pieces.
4. In a skillet, melt the butter over medium heat. Add the shallots and cook for 2-3 minutes until softened.
5. Add the brandy and cook for 2 minutes until the alcohol evaporates.
6. Stir in the heavy cream, then add the lobster meat and cook for another 2 minutes.
7. Season with salt, pepper, and parsley.
8. Stuff the lobster shells with the mixture, sprinkle with Gruyère, and top with breadcrumbs if using.
9. Bake for 10-12 minutes, until the cheese is melted and golden.

Brie and Mushroom Stuffed Beef Wellington

Ingredients:

- 2 lb beef tenderloin
- 1/2 lb mushrooms, finely chopped
- 2 tbsp butter
- 2 tbsp olive oil
- 4 oz Brie cheese, sliced
- 1 sheet puff pastry
- 1 egg, beaten (for egg wash)
- Salt and pepper to taste

Instructions:

1. Preheat the oven to 400°F (200°C).
2. Heat olive oil in a pan and sear the beef tenderloin on all sides. Season with salt and pepper.
3. In the same pan, melt butter and sauté the mushrooms until softened and the moisture evaporates.
4. Lay the puff pastry on a sheet of parchment paper. Place the Brie cheese slices in the center, then spread the sautéed mushrooms on top.
5. Place the seared beef on the mushrooms and fold the pastry around it.
6. Brush the pastry with the beaten egg and bake for 25-30 minutes, until the pastry is golden and the beef reaches your desired level of doneness.
7. Let it rest for 10 minutes before slicing and serving.

Grilled Cheese with Caramelized Onion and Gruyère

Ingredients:

- 2 slices sourdough bread
- 4 oz Gruyère cheese, sliced
- 1/2 onion, thinly sliced
- 1 tbsp butter
- 1 tbsp olive oil
- Salt and pepper to taste

Instructions:

1. In a skillet, heat the butter and olive oil over medium heat. Add the onion and cook for 15-20 minutes, stirring occasionally, until caramelized.
2. Butter one side of each slice of bread.
3. Layer one slice of bread with Gruyère cheese and caramelized onions, then top with the other slice of bread, butter side out.
4. Grill the sandwich over medium heat until golden brown on both sides and the cheese is melted, about 3-4 minutes per side.
5. Serve warm and enjoy!

Baked Ziti with Ricotta and Mozzarella

Ingredients:

- 12 oz ziti pasta
- 2 cups ricotta cheese
- 1 1/2 cups mozzarella cheese, shredded
- 1/2 cup Parmesan cheese, grated
- 2 cups marinara sauce
- 1 egg, beaten
- 2 tbsp fresh basil, chopped
- Salt and pepper to taste

Instructions:

1. Preheat the oven to 375°F (190°C).
2. Cook the ziti pasta according to package directions. Drain and set aside.
3. In a bowl, mix the ricotta, half of the mozzarella, Parmesan, egg, basil, salt, and pepper.
4. Combine the cooked pasta with the cheese mixture and marinara sauce.
5. Transfer the mixture to a baking dish, top with the remaining mozzarella, and bake for 20-25 minutes, until bubbly and golden.
6. Serve hot.

Macaroni and Cheese with Smoked Gouda

Ingredients:

- 8 oz elbow macaroni
- 2 tbsp butter
- 2 tbsp flour
- 1 1/2 cups milk
- 1 cup smoked Gouda cheese, shredded
- 1/2 cup sharp cheddar cheese, shredded
- 1 tsp Dijon mustard
- Salt and pepper to taste
- 1/4 cup breadcrumbs (optional)

Instructions:

1. Cook the macaroni according to package directions. Drain and set aside.
2. In a saucepan, melt the butter over medium heat. Stir in the flour and cook for 1-2 minutes.
3. Gradually whisk in the milk and cook until the sauce thickens.
4. Stir in the Gouda, cheddar, and Dijon mustard until smooth. Season with salt and pepper.
5. Toss the cooked pasta in the cheese sauce and transfer to a baking dish.
6. Top with breadcrumbs if desired, and bake at 375°F (190°C) for 10-12 minutes, until golden.

Ricotta and Spinach Gnocchi

Ingredients:

- 1 1/2 cups ricotta cheese
- 1/2 cup spinach, cooked and squeezed dry
- 1 1/2 cups all-purpose flour
- 1 egg
- 1/4 tsp nutmeg
- Salt and pepper to taste
- 1/4 cup Parmesan cheese, grated

Instructions:

1. In a bowl, combine the ricotta, spinach, egg, flour, nutmeg, salt, and pepper. Mix until a dough forms.
2. Roll the dough into long ropes and cut into bite-sized pieces.
3. Bring a pot of salted water to a boil. Drop the gnocchi into the water and cook for 2-3 minutes, until they float to the surface.
4. Remove with a slotted spoon and toss with melted butter and Parmesan. Serve hot.

Parmesan-Crusted Halibut

Ingredients:

- 4 halibut fillets
- 1 cup grated Parmesan cheese
- 1/2 cup panko breadcrumbs
- 2 tbsp fresh parsley, chopped
- 1/2 tsp garlic powder
- 1/2 tsp lemon zest
- Salt and pepper to taste
- 2 tbsp olive oil

Instructions:

1. Preheat the oven to 400°F (200°C).
2. In a bowl, combine Parmesan, panko, parsley, garlic powder, lemon zest, salt, and pepper.
3. Season halibut fillets with salt and pepper, then coat them with the Parmesan mixture.
4. Heat olive oil in a skillet over medium heat. Sear the fillets for 2 minutes on each side.
5. Transfer the fillets to a baking sheet and bake for 6-8 minutes, or until the fish is cooked through and the crust is golden.
6. Serve hot, garnished with extra parsley.

Manchego and Quince Jam Crostini

Ingredients:

- 1 baguette, sliced
- 4 oz Manchego cheese, sliced
- 3 tbsp quince jam
- Olive oil for brushing
- Fresh thyme for garnish

Instructions:

1. Preheat the oven to 375°F (190°C).
2. Brush baguette slices with olive oil and bake for 8-10 minutes, or until crispy.
3. Spread quince jam on each crostini.
4. Top with a slice of Manchego cheese and return to the oven for 3-4 minutes until the cheese is just melted.
5. Garnish with fresh thyme and serve immediately.

Mozzarella di Bufala with Roasted Tomatoes

Ingredients:

- 8 oz fresh mozzarella di bufala, sliced
- 1 pint cherry tomatoes, halved
- 2 tbsp olive oil
- 1 tbsp balsamic vinegar
- Fresh basil leaves
- Salt and pepper to taste

Instructions:

1. Preheat the oven to 375°F (190°C).
2. Toss cherry tomatoes with olive oil, salt, and pepper, and roast on a baking sheet for 15-20 minutes, until softened.
3. Arrange the mozzarella slices on a platter, topping with roasted tomatoes.
4. Drizzle with balsamic vinegar and garnish with fresh basil leaves.
5. Serve immediately, seasoned with extra salt and pepper to taste.

Burrata with Fresh Basil and Olive Oil

Ingredients:

- 1 ball burrata cheese
- Fresh basil leaves
- 2 tbsp extra virgin olive oil
- Salt and pepper to taste

Instructions:

1. Place the burrata on a serving dish.
2. Drizzle with olive oil and sprinkle with salt and pepper.
3. Garnish with fresh basil leaves.
4. Serve with crusty bread or crackers for dipping.

Truffle and Parmesan Fries

Ingredients:

- 4 large russet potatoes, cut into fries
- 2 tbsp truffle oil
- 1/2 cup Parmesan cheese, grated
- Fresh parsley, chopped
- Salt to taste

Instructions:

1. Preheat the oven to 425°F (220°C).
2. Toss the fries in olive oil and season with salt. Spread them on a baking sheet.
3. Bake for 30-35 minutes, flipping halfway, until crispy and golden.
4. Drizzle with truffle oil and sprinkle with Parmesan and parsley before serving.

Stuffed Piquillo Peppers with Goat Cheese

Ingredients:

- 12 piquillo peppers, drained
- 4 oz goat cheese
- 1 tbsp fresh thyme, chopped
- 1 tbsp olive oil
- Salt and pepper to taste

Instructions:

1. Preheat the oven to 375°F (190°C).
2. Mix goat cheese with thyme, salt, and pepper.
3. Stuff each piquillo pepper with the goat cheese mixture.
4. Arrange stuffed peppers on a baking sheet, drizzle with olive oil, and bake for 12-15 minutes.
5. Serve warm.

Cheddar and Ale Soup

Ingredients:

- 2 tbsp butter
- 1 onion, chopped
- 2 cloves garlic, minced
- 1/4 cup all-purpose flour
- 2 cups chicken broth
- 2 cups whole milk
- 1 1/2 cups sharp cheddar cheese, shredded
- 1/2 cup ale
- Salt and pepper to taste

Instructions:

1. Melt butter in a large pot over medium heat. Add onion and garlic, cooking until softened.
2. Stir in the flour and cook for 2 minutes.
3. Gradually add the chicken broth and milk, whisking constantly.
4. Bring to a simmer and cook for 10 minutes until thickened.
5. Stir in the cheese and ale, and cook until the cheese has melted.
6. Season with salt and pepper, and serve hot.

Burrata and Prosciutto Salad

Ingredients:

- 2 cups mixed greens
- 1 ball burrata cheese
- 4 slices prosciutto
- 1 tbsp balsamic glaze
- Olive oil for drizzling
- Salt and pepper to taste

Instructions:

1. Arrange mixed greens on a plate.
2. Tear the burrata into pieces and scatter over the greens.
3. Drape the prosciutto over the salad.
4. Drizzle with olive oil and balsamic glaze.
5. Season with salt and pepper, and serve immediately.

Feta and Olive Tapenade on Crostini

Ingredients:

- 1 cup pitted Kalamata olives, chopped
- 1/4 cup feta cheese, crumbled
- 1 tbsp capers, chopped
- 2 tbsp olive oil
- 1 clove garlic, minced
- 1 tbsp fresh parsley, chopped
- 1 baguette, sliced

Instructions:

1. Preheat the oven to 375°F (190°C).
2. Brush baguette slices with olive oil and bake for 8-10 minutes until crispy.
3. Mix chopped olives, feta, capers, garlic, and parsley in a bowl.
4. Top each crostini with the feta and olive tapenade mixture.
5. Serve immediately.

Goat Cheese and Beets Salad

Ingredients:

- 2 medium beets, roasted and sliced
- 4 oz goat cheese, crumbled
- 4 cups mixed greens (arugula, spinach, or mesclun)
- 1/4 cup walnuts, toasted
- 2 tbsp balsamic vinaigrette
- Salt and pepper to taste

Instructions:

1. Roast the beets by wrapping them in foil and baking at 400°F (200°C) for 45-60 minutes until tender. Peel and slice.
2. In a large bowl, toss the greens, beets, goat cheese, and toasted walnuts.
3. Drizzle with balsamic vinaigrette and season with salt and pepper.
4. Serve immediately.

Creamy Spinach and Feta Dip

Ingredients:

- 1 cup frozen spinach, thawed and drained
- 8 oz cream cheese, softened
- 1/2 cup sour cream
- 1/2 cup feta cheese, crumbled
- 1/4 cup Parmesan cheese, grated
- 1 clove garlic, minced
- 1 tbsp lemon juice
- Salt and pepper to taste

Instructions:

1. Preheat the oven to 375°F (190°C).
2. In a mixing bowl, combine cream cheese, sour cream, feta, Parmesan, garlic, lemon juice, and spinach.
3. Season with salt and pepper and mix until smooth.
4. Transfer to a baking dish and bake for 20 minutes, until bubbly and golden on top.
5. Serve with pita, crackers, or vegetables for dipping.

Lobster and Shrimp Macaroni and Cheese

Ingredients:

- 1 lb lobster meat, cooked and chopped
- 1/2 lb shrimp, peeled and deveined
- 8 oz elbow macaroni
- 2 tbsp butter
- 1/4 cup flour
- 2 cups whole milk
- 1 cup sharp cheddar cheese, shredded
- 1/2 cup Gruyère cheese, shredded
- Salt and pepper to taste
- 1/4 tsp paprika

Instructions:

1. Cook macaroni according to package instructions and set aside.
2. In a large skillet, melt butter over medium heat. Add flour and whisk to form a roux.
3. Gradually add milk, whisking constantly until thickened.
4. Stir in cheddar, Gruyère, salt, pepper, and paprika, cooking until the cheese is melted.
5. Add lobster, shrimp, and cooked macaroni to the skillet. Stir to combine.
6. Serve hot, garnished with extra paprika if desired.

Chicken Parmesan with Fresh Mozzarella

Ingredients:

- 4 chicken breasts, boneless and skinless
- 1 cup breadcrumbs
- 1/2 cup grated Parmesan cheese
- 1 egg, beaten
- 2 cups marinara sauce
- 1 ball fresh mozzarella, sliced
- 2 tbsp olive oil
- Fresh basil for garnish

Instructions:

1. Preheat the oven to 375°F (190°C).
2. In a shallow dish, combine breadcrumbs and Parmesan. Dip chicken breasts into beaten egg, then coat in breadcrumb mixture.
3. Heat olive oil in a skillet over medium heat. Brown chicken breasts for 4-5 minutes on each side.
4. Transfer chicken to a baking dish. Top each breast with marinara sauce and mozzarella slices.
5. Bake for 20 minutes, or until the chicken is cooked through and the cheese is melted.
6. Garnish with fresh basil and serve hot.

Grilled Halloumi with Lemon and Mint

Ingredients:

- 8 oz halloumi cheese, sliced
- 1 tbsp olive oil
- 1 tbsp lemon juice
- 1 tbsp fresh mint, chopped
- Salt and pepper to taste

Instructions:

1. Preheat a grill or grill pan over medium heat.
2. Brush halloumi slices with olive oil and grill for 2-3 minutes per side, until golden and crispy.
3. Drizzle with lemon juice and sprinkle with fresh mint.
4. Season with salt and pepper, then serve immediately.

Baked Eggplant Parmesan with Fresh Mozzarella

Ingredients:

- 2 medium eggplants, sliced
- 1 1/2 cups marinara sauce
- 1 cup breadcrumbs
- 1/2 cup grated Parmesan cheese
- 2 balls fresh mozzarella, sliced
- 1 egg, beaten
- 1/4 cup fresh basil, chopped
- Olive oil for drizzling

Instructions:

1. Preheat the oven to 375°F (190°C).
2. Dip eggplant slices in beaten egg, then coat in breadcrumbs mixed with Parmesan.
3. Arrange eggplant slices on a baking sheet and drizzle with olive oil. Bake for 25-30 minutes, flipping halfway, until crispy.
4. In a baking dish, layer eggplant slices with marinara sauce and fresh mozzarella.
5. Bake for an additional 15 minutes, until the cheese is melted.
6. Garnish with fresh basil and serve hot.

Sweet Potato and Goat Cheese Tart

Ingredients:

- 1 sheet puff pastry
- 2 medium sweet potatoes, peeled and thinly sliced
- 4 oz goat cheese, crumbled
- 1 tbsp olive oil
- 1 tbsp honey
- Fresh thyme for garnish
- Salt and pepper to taste

Instructions:

1. Preheat the oven to 400°F (200°C).
2. Roll out the puff pastry on a baking sheet and score a border around the edges.
3. Arrange sweet potato slices over the pastry, drizzle with olive oil, and season with salt and pepper.
4. Bake for 20 minutes, then remove from the oven and sprinkle with goat cheese.
5. Drizzle with honey and return to the oven for another 10 minutes, until golden.
6. Garnish with fresh thyme and serve immediately.

Ricotta and Lemon Cannoli

Ingredients:

- 12 cannoli shells
- 1 1/2 cups ricotta cheese
- 1/2 cup powdered sugar
- Zest of 1 lemon
- 1/2 tsp vanilla extract
- 1/4 cup mini chocolate chips
- 1/4 cup crushed pistachios

Instructions:

1. In a bowl, combine ricotta, powdered sugar, lemon zest, and vanilla extract. Stir until smooth.
2. Using a piping bag, fill each cannoli shell with the ricotta mixture.
3. Sprinkle the ends of the filled shells with chocolate chips and crushed pistachios.
4. Serve immediately or refrigerate until ready to serve.

Roquefort and Walnut Salad

Ingredients:

- 4 cups mixed greens
- 2 oz Roquefort cheese, crumbled
- 1/4 cup walnuts, toasted
- 1/4 red onion, thinly sliced
- 1 tbsp olive oil
- 1 tbsp balsamic vinegar
- Salt and pepper to taste

Instructions:

1. In a large bowl, combine mixed greens, Roquefort, walnuts, and red onion.
2. Drizzle with olive oil and balsamic vinegar.
3. Toss gently to combine and season with salt and pepper.
4. Serve immediately.

Grilled Steak with Blue Cheese Butter

Ingredients:

- 2 steaks (ribeye, sirloin, or your choice)
- 2 tbsp butter, softened
- 2 oz blue cheese, crumbled
- 1 clove garlic, minced
- 1 tsp fresh parsley, chopped
- Salt and pepper to taste
- Olive oil for grilling

Instructions:

1. Preheat your grill or grill pan to medium-high heat.
2. Season the steaks with salt, pepper, and a drizzle of olive oil.
3. Grill steaks for 4-6 minutes per side (for medium-rare), or until desired doneness.
4. While the steaks are grilling, mix softened butter, blue cheese, garlic, and parsley in a bowl.
5. Once the steaks are cooked, place a dollop of the blue cheese butter on top of each steak.
6. Let the butter melt over the steak and serve immediately.

Moussaka with Feta Cheese

Ingredients:

- 2 eggplants, sliced
- 1 lb ground lamb or beef
- 1 onion, chopped
- 2 cloves garlic, minced
- 1 can (14 oz) crushed tomatoes
- 1/4 cup red wine (optional)
- 1 tsp ground cinnamon
- 1 tsp dried oregano
- 1/2 tsp ground nutmeg
- 2 tbsp olive oil
- Salt and pepper to taste
- 2 cups béchamel sauce
- 1 cup feta cheese, crumbled
- 1/4 cup grated Parmesan cheese

Instructions:

1. Preheat the oven to 375°F (190°C).
2. Slice eggplants and roast or fry them lightly with olive oil until soft and golden brown. Set aside.
3. In a skillet, heat olive oil and cook onions and garlic until soft. Add the ground meat and brown.
4. Add crushed tomatoes, red wine (if using), cinnamon, oregano, nutmeg, salt, and pepper. Simmer for 10 minutes.
5. In a baking dish, layer the cooked eggplant, then the meat mixture, and top with béchamel sauce.
6. Sprinkle with crumbled feta and Parmesan cheese.
7. Bake for 30-40 minutes until golden and bubbly. Let cool for 10 minutes before serving.

Ricotta and Spinach Stuffed Chicken Breast

Ingredients:

- 4 boneless, skinless chicken breasts
- 1 cup ricotta cheese
- 1/2 cup fresh spinach, chopped
- 1/4 cup Parmesan cheese, grated
- 1 clove garlic, minced
- 1 tsp dried oregano
- Salt and pepper to taste
- 1 tbsp olive oil
- 1 cup marinara sauce (optional)

Instructions:

1. Preheat the oven to 375°F (190°C).
2. In a bowl, mix ricotta, spinach, Parmesan, garlic, oregano, salt, and pepper.
3. Cut a pocket into each chicken breast and stuff with the ricotta-spinach mixture.
4. Heat olive oil in a skillet over medium heat. Brown the chicken on both sides for 2-3 minutes each.
5. Transfer the chicken to a baking dish and bake for 20-25 minutes until cooked through.
6. Serve with marinara sauce if desired.

Cheese-Stuffed Poblano Peppers

Ingredients:

- 4 poblano peppers
- 1 cup shredded Monterey Jack cheese
- 1/2 cup cream cheese, softened
- 1/4 cup grated Parmesan cheese
- 1 tsp cumin
- Salt and pepper to taste
- Olive oil for brushing

Instructions:

1. Preheat the oven to 400°F (200°C).
2. Slice the poblano peppers in half and remove the seeds.
3. In a bowl, mix Monterey Jack, cream cheese, Parmesan, cumin, salt, and pepper.
4. Stuff the peppers with the cheese mixture.
5. Place the stuffed peppers on a baking sheet and brush lightly with olive oil.
6. Roast in the oven for 20-25 minutes until the peppers are tender and the cheese is melted and golden.
7. Serve immediately.

Focaccia with Ricotta and Honey

Ingredients:

- 1 lb pizza dough
- 1/2 cup ricotta cheese
- 2 tbsp honey
- 1/4 cup olive oil
- Fresh rosemary, chopped
- Salt to taste

Instructions:

1. Preheat the oven to 375°F (190°C).
2. Roll out the pizza dough on a baking sheet.
3. Brush with olive oil and press dimples into the dough using your fingers.
4. Spread ricotta cheese evenly over the dough.
5. Drizzle with honey and sprinkle with fresh rosemary.
6. Bake for 15-20 minutes until golden and crispy.
7. Sprinkle with a pinch of salt before serving.

Parmesan and Herb-Crusted Chicken

Ingredients:

- 4 boneless chicken breasts
- 1 cup breadcrumbs
- 1/2 cup grated Parmesan cheese
- 1 tbsp fresh thyme, chopped
- 1 tbsp fresh rosemary, chopped
- 1 egg, beaten
- Salt and pepper to taste
- Olive oil for frying

Instructions:

1. Preheat the oven to 375°F (190°C).
2. In a shallow bowl, combine breadcrumbs, Parmesan, thyme, rosemary, salt, and pepper.
3. Dip each chicken breast into the beaten egg, then coat in the breadcrumb mixture.
4. Heat olive oil in a skillet over medium heat. Brown the chicken on both sides for 2-3 minutes each.
5. Transfer the chicken to a baking dish and bake for 20-25 minutes until cooked through.
6. Serve with a side of vegetables or salad.

Truffle Gouda Risotto

Ingredients:

- 1 1/2 cups Arborio rice
- 4 cups chicken or vegetable broth
- 1/2 cup white wine
- 1 small onion, chopped
- 2 tbsp butter
- 1/2 cup Gouda cheese, shredded
- 1 tbsp truffle oil
- 1/4 cup Parmesan cheese, grated
- Salt and pepper to taste

Instructions:

1. In a saucepan, bring broth to a simmer and keep warm.
2. In a separate large pan, melt butter over medium heat and sauté the onion until translucent.
3. Add the Arborio rice and stir until lightly toasted.
4. Pour in the white wine and cook until absorbed.
5. Gradually add the warm broth, one ladle at a time, stirring constantly and letting each addition absorb before adding more. Continue until the rice is tender and creamy, about 18-20 minutes.
6. Stir in the Gouda, Parmesan, and truffle oil. Season with salt and pepper.
7. Serve hot, garnished with extra cheese or fresh herbs.

Prosciutto and Brie Croissants

Ingredients:

- 4 croissants, sliced in half
- 4 oz Brie cheese, sliced
- 4 oz prosciutto, thinly sliced
- 1 tbsp Dijon mustard
- 1 tbsp honey (optional)
- Fresh arugula or spinach (optional)

Instructions:

1. Preheat the oven to 350°F (175°C).
2. Slice the croissants in half lengthwise.
3. Spread a thin layer of Dijon mustard and honey (if using) on the bottom half of each croissant.
4. Layer Brie cheese, prosciutto, and arugula (if using) on top.
5. Place the top half of the croissant on the filled bottom half.
6. Bake the croissants for 10-12 minutes or until the cheese is melted and the croissant is golden brown.
7. Serve immediately.

Poached Pears with Gorgonzola and Walnuts

Ingredients:

- 4 pears, peeled and halved
- 1 cup red wine
- 1/2 cup water
- 1/4 cup sugar
- 1 tsp vanilla extract
- 4 oz Gorgonzola cheese, crumbled
- 1/4 cup walnuts, toasted and chopped
- Fresh thyme or rosemary for garnish

Instructions:

1. In a saucepan, combine red wine, water, sugar, and vanilla extract. Bring to a simmer over medium heat.
2. Add the pear halves and cook for 15-20 minutes until tender, turning the pears occasionally.
3. Remove the pears from the liquid and set aside.
4. Reduce the poaching liquid by half until it becomes a syrup-like consistency.
5. Plate the poached pears and drizzle with the reduced syrup.
6. Top with crumbled Gorgonzola cheese, chopped walnuts, and fresh thyme or rosemary.
7. Serve warm or at room temperature.

Sautéed Shrimp with Garlic and Parmesan

Ingredients:

- 1 lb large shrimp, peeled and deveined
- 3 tbsp olive oil
- 3 cloves garlic, minced
- 1/4 cup Parmesan cheese, grated
- 1 tbsp fresh parsley, chopped
- Salt and pepper to taste
- Lemon wedges for serving

Instructions:

1. Heat olive oil in a large skillet over medium-high heat.
2. Add the garlic and sauté for 1 minute until fragrant.
3. Add the shrimp to the pan, season with salt and pepper, and sauté for 2-3 minutes on each side until pink and cooked through.
4. Remove the shrimp from the skillet and sprinkle with grated Parmesan and fresh parsley.
5. Serve with lemon wedges.

Grilled Veggie and Goat Cheese Sandwich

Ingredients:

- 2 slices rustic bread or sourdough
- 1/4 cup goat cheese, softened
- 1/2 zucchini, sliced
- 1/2 bell pepper, sliced
- 1/2 red onion, sliced
- 1 tbsp olive oil
- Salt and pepper to taste
- Fresh basil (optional)

Instructions:

1. Preheat a grill pan or outdoor grill.
2. Toss the zucchini, bell pepper, and onion in olive oil and season with salt and pepper.
3. Grill the vegetables for 5-7 minutes, turning occasionally until tender and lightly charred.
4. While the veggies are grilling, spread goat cheese on one side of each slice of bread.
5. Once the veggies are done, assemble the sandwich by layering grilled veggies on one slice of bread.
6. Top with fresh basil (optional) and place the other slice of bread on top.
7. Grill the sandwich on both sides until golden and crispy.
8. Serve hot.

Baked Polenta with Blue Cheese and Mushrooms

Ingredients:

- 1 cup instant polenta
- 3 cups vegetable or chicken broth
- 1 tbsp butter
- 1/2 cup blue cheese, crumbled
- 1 cup mushrooms, sliced
- 1 tbsp olive oil
- Salt and pepper to taste

Instructions:

1. Preheat the oven to 375°F (190°C).
2. In a saucepan, bring the broth to a boil. Gradually whisk in the polenta and cook until thickened, about 5 minutes.
3. Stir in butter, blue cheese, salt, and pepper.
4. Pour the polenta mixture into a greased baking dish and bake for 20 minutes.
5. While the polenta is baking, heat olive oil in a skillet and sauté the mushrooms until golden brown and tender, about 5-7 minutes.
6. Once the polenta is baked, top with sautéed mushrooms and additional crumbled blue cheese.
7. Serve warm.

Crab Cakes with Parmesan Cream Sauce

Ingredients:

- 1 lb crab meat, drained
- 1/4 cup breadcrumbs
- 1 egg, beaten
- 1/4 cup mayonnaise
- 2 tbsp Dijon mustard
- 1 tbsp fresh parsley, chopped
- 1 tbsp lemon juice
- Salt and pepper to taste
- Olive oil for frying

For the Parmesan Cream Sauce:

- 1/2 cup heavy cream
- 1/4 cup Parmesan cheese, grated
- 1 tbsp butter
- Salt and pepper to taste

Instructions:

1. In a bowl, combine crab meat, breadcrumbs, egg, mayonnaise, Dijon mustard, parsley, lemon juice, salt, and pepper. Mix well.
2. Form the mixture into 8 small patties.
3. Heat olive oil in a skillet over medium-high heat. Fry the crab cakes for 3-4 minutes per side until golden brown.
4. While the crab cakes are cooking, prepare the sauce by heating heavy cream and butter in a saucepan over medium heat.
5. Once the cream begins to simmer, stir in Parmesan cheese and cook until thickened, about 3-4 minutes. Season with salt and pepper.
6. Serve the crab cakes with a drizzle of Parmesan cream sauce.